Alex the AWESOME & THE CRAZY QUEST FOR THE GOLDEN POD

First edition published in 2019
by Everything Slight Pepper.
P.O. Box 1373 Wrightson Road
Port of Spain, Trinidad and Tobago.

ISBN: 978-976-95350-3-9

Concept & layout by **Jeunanne Alkins**
Written by **Jeunanne Alkins & Janine Mendes-Franco**
Illustrations by **Cria Ideias**
Typesetting by **Stephanie Telemaque**
Edited by **Karel Mc Intosh**

A very special thank you to Isabel Brash (Cocobel Chocolates), The Alliance of Rural Communities and Leif Johnson (Carmel Valley Estate) for teaching us about cocoa and where chocolate comes from.

PRINTED IN CHINA

www.wearebrighteyed.com @wearebrighteyed

If you're coming with me on this mission,
the first thing you have to realise is that...

Nothing is
AS IT SEEMS...

Me? I look like a tailless rat, but cuter. People underestimate me all the time, but I can gnaw my way through hard surfaces better than a nutcracker and I can sniff out danger a mile away. Plus, I have a penchant for the finer things in life, which is why we're here.

Where exactly is here? This estate is in the middle of tropical rainforest, which must mean that we're close to **the alligator?**

oops, no,

the detonator?

oops, no, that's not right...

Wait.
I've got it!

We're close to the equator!
Map of the world
North America
Europe
Equator
Caribbean
Africa
South America
Cocoa Rainforest
TOP SECRET
ADDRESS:
Tree Trunk No. 9
Theobroma Estate

The Equator is an imaginary line across the earth, which divides it into two, equal parts.

These types of forests only grow in warmer countries closer to the equator.

See those trees over there with the broad leaves?

Yes, the ones with clusters of tiny, white and pink flowers on their trunk and branches. I've been keeping an eye on them from my burrow. The flowers have been morphing bit by bit, into small pods.

That's the treasure we're after!

Not much of a challenge, you say?
Where's the fun of treasure hiding
in plain sight?
What kind of tree
sprouts fruit
from its
trunk?!

COCOA!

As the pods have been growing, they have become large and full. Sometimes they're deep red or dark purple, other times, they're bright yellow and blazing orange, like glowing suns.

Cocoa cannot be easily picked.
If you pull the pod and remove the whole branch with it, you'll do serious damage. A new pod will never be able to grow in that spot again! You have to gently turn it so that you don't break off the part that's attached to the trunk. On the cocoa estate, there is so much to pick that the farmers made a weapon to make the job easier.

Look at it over there.
It is called a gullet rod or cocoa knife.
They've attached a sharp, metal blade to the end of a long bamboo rod and use it to pick the pods that are out of reach.
Wait a minute...what are those humans doing?

Are they picking green pods?

Are they crazy?

Those aren’t ripe.
They're going to spoil the whole batch!
We’ve got to stop them!
You think we should wait? Secret agents don’t wait.
They spring into action!
Hiiii
YAHHHH!

Wait, what's that?
They're talking about the green pods...
they are saying that they are ripe!?
Impossible!

They're a special type of cocoa called what?

Moustachio?

oops, no, **Pistachio?**

oops, no, that's not right...

Wait. I've got it!

Trinitario!

It seems that the Trinitario pods can be ripe in a variety of colours! If they're right, this might be the most valuable pod of all, and... it's not always golden!

CLUE
FOSTERO +
CRIOLO
= TRINITARIO

Let's see what inside this one looks like. Go ahead, give it a whack!

Not as easy as it looks, is it? Try again.

There, YOU DID IT!

That's the beauty of cocoa. If you want it, you're going to have to work for it. Do you know how many creatures want to taste the seeds, but just can't get the pod open? That's where my super-strong teeth come in. LOOK! The beans are surrounded by creamy pulp.

You're not afraid of a little gooeyness, are you?

Mmmmm, **the pulp is sweet!**

I hear voices. **Quick! Let's go!**

The farmers are splitting the cocoa pods open by bashing them against a hard surface and twisting some open with a knife in one, smooth motion.

Then they're scooping out the pulpy seeds by hand.
What's that now? Where are they taking them?
The seeds have to go into Wet SOCKS?
Wait. No!
that's not right!

It's a SWEAT BOX!

They keep the beans in wooden boxes for about a week to ferment, covering them with banana leaves for extra padding. The heat makes the pulp turn into squishy juices that drain away between the spaces at the bottom.

The farmers then spread the beans with wooden rakes, to dry in the open air, but they have to be on the lookout for rain. This estate already has it covered!

Behold, a Cocoa house!
It looks just like a normal house, except it's on stilts and...

...the roof **CAN MOVE!**

It sits on wheels so that the farmers can roll it back and forth, to uncover the beans for drying and cover the floor when it rains.

Wait, do you hear **music?**

I hope you've got moves, because we're going to **DANCE the COCOA!**

The farmers sprinkle water on the dried beans to get rid of any leftover bits, then polish them with their bare feet to make the beans shiny!

As our feet shuffle,
the beans dazzle!

GO AGENTS
GO GO AGENTS!
GO
GO
GO AGENTS!!!

Oh no! The farmers and their pesky dogs.
They have spotted us! Quick, find us a good hiding spot while I fend them off with my expert moves.
When the going gets TOUGH...
the TOUGH get GOING!
Let's GO!

Phew; that was close! But at least we got away, and now we can get back to... wait a minute... this hideout is shaking! It's alive! How can a mound of cocoa sacks move?

What? We're on a moving truck!

Where are we going!?!

Shhh...do you hear voices?
Does something else happen after the beans leave the estate?

Wait a minute...they're talking about roasting them to separate the husks from the inner beans, and make cracking them easier.
We need to get out of here!
Roasted AGOUTI is NOT on the menu!

That was close. **Those are big ovens!** It's beginning to smell a lot like something delicious!

What is going on over there now? Whinnying? **Like a horse?** No, wait. I've got it! **Winnowing!** It means to blow the husk away from the beans, leaving only the cocoa nibs behind.

She's grinding the nibs into a liquid, called cocoa liquor and then adding other ingredients like sugar, milk, and cocoa butter. **Wow, that's a lot of mixing! It's called conching...** no, not like the huge seashell! She is using this machine to keep mixing everything until she's happy with the texture.

To set it properly, she is **tempering** the mixture, which crystallises the cocoa butter, by stirring and cooling the mix to a specific temperature at the same time.

It's beginning **to look a lot like...**

But you're right, my trusty sidekick. It doesn't look finished. The chocolate still has to take shape. She's pouring the liquid into molds, so that it hardens into a pattern when it cools.

Okay, get ready. As soon as she leaves, we are going in for a taste test.

NOM
nom NOM!
Nom nom
chocolate NOM
nom chocolate
NOM NOM nom
NOM CHOCOLATE!

SECRET AGENT INTELLIGENCE REPORT

WEAPONS FOUND:

Cocoa Knife
"Gullet Rod"
(Official Name)

Wooden Shovel & Rake

Sweat Box

SKILLS LEARNED:

Fermenting
Roasting
Winnowing
Conching
Tempering

CLASSIFIED INFORMATION UNCOVERED:

1- Chocolate is made from a fruit named Cocoa that grows on trees. The Latin name for cocoa is Theobroma, which translates into "food of the gods".

2- There are three types of cocoa: Criollo, Forastero and Trinitario. Trinitario is a hybrid of the first two and was created in Trinidad.

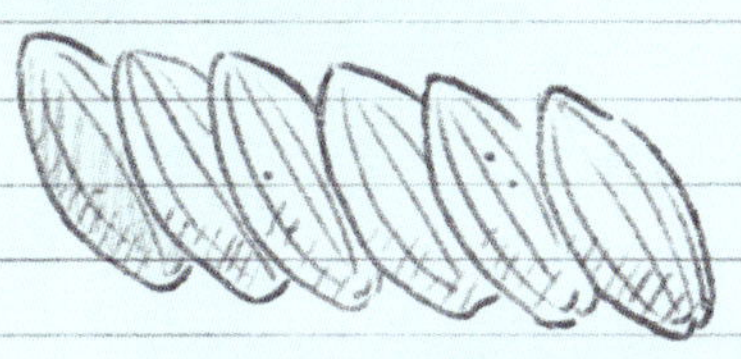

3- Ripe Trinitario cocoa pods can be a variety of colours: yellow, orange, purple, maroon and even green!

4- The pulp around the beans is creamy and sweet, but the raw beans actually taste bitter!

5- The Cocoa House has a movable roof which is rolled back and forth over the drying beds to either let in the sun or keep out the rain.

6- The beans are kept on the drying beds for about a week, or until they are reduced to about 7% moisture.

7- Dancing the Cocoa is a tradition to remove excess dried pulp and polish the beans with your bare feet to make them shiny.

8- It takes about 400 cocoa beans to make one pound of chocolate.

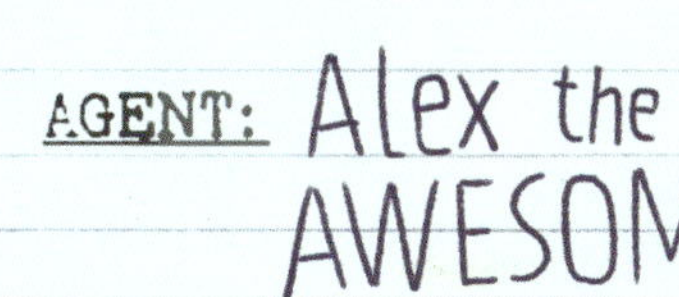

AGENT: Alex the AWESOME